Fast
Vegetarian

KÖNEMANN

❖ FAST VEGETARIAN ❖

The Vegetarian Kitchen

While a balanced vegetarian diet has many proven health benefits, when you're cooking on the go, juggling nutrients can seem a chore. It need not be if you stock your pantry with a variety of vegetarian 'power' foods such as cereals, nuts and pulses.

A balanced vegetarian diet is typically low in fat yet high in complex carbohydrates, fiber, vitamins and minerals—a combination that has been shown to guard against many diseases.

However, simply cutting out meat does not guarantee a healthy diet. As with any diet, you need to eat a wide variety of fresh foods and little processed or 'junk' food. Vegetarian diets also need planning to prevent deficiencies in protein, vitamin B_{12}, iron, zinc and calcium.

There are two main types of vegetarians. 'Lacto-vegetarians' will consume certain animal products such as milk products and eggs. 'Vegans' consume only plant products, and because they eat no eggs or dairy products, are more susceptible to deficiencies in protein,

calcium and vitamin B_{12}.

Protein deficiency is rare in vegetarians who regularly eat eggs and milk products. Vegans need to combine plant proteins to get enough protein—some good combinations include: cereals with legumes; cereals and vegetables; cereals with nuts and seeds; legumes and vegetables; legumes with nuts or seeds.

Calcium and zinc are poorly absorbed from plant sources, so all vegetarians need to eat plenty of foods rich in these nutrients, and also in vitamin B_{12}—a vitamin mostly found in animal meats.

All vegetarians (especially women and teenage girls) also need to eat a lot of iron-rich plant foods. To increase the absorption of iron from these sources, incorporate vitamin C into the meal.

CALCIUM
Needed for: Strong bones and teeth.
Found in: Milk products; figs; parsley; natural granola; brazil nuts; fortified soy milk; tofu; soya beans; miso; dehusked tahini; almonds; pistachio nuts; chickpeas; sunflower seeds; spinach; kelp.

VITAMIN B12
Needed for: Healthy nerve tissue. **Found in:** Cheese; sauerkraut; miso; yogurt; eggs; milk; tempeh; tofu; mushrooms.

PROTEIN
Needed for: Growth of all body tissues. **Found in:** Lentils; peas; beans; cereal grains such as brown rice, couscous and bulghur wheat; milk products; seeds; soya products such as tofu and tempeh; eggs; nuts; chickpeas; sprouts.

2

IRON

Needed to: Carry oxygen around the body. **Found in:** Dried apricots, pears and peaches; raisins; cereal grains such as bulghur wheat, couscous and polenta; whole-wheat pasta and bread; green vegetables; tofu; bran flakes; rice bran; baked beans; pumpkin and sunflower seeds.

ZINC

Needed to: Absorb other vitamins. **Found in:** Wheat germ; pecans; soya beans; cashews; rice bran; pine nuts; brazil nuts; sesame seeds; sunflower seeds.

Fast Vegetarian

Fast food doesn't have to mean junk food. It can mean energy-giving dishes in an instant: food that is fresh in flavor, big on style, and superbly nourishing, too—perfect for busy people hungry for a hearty feast, or just a light meal.

Fragrant Paella

Ready to eat in
* 30 minutes*
Serves 4–6

5 cups vegetable stock
good pinch of saffron
* threads or 1/4 teaspoon*
* saffron powder*
2 tablespoons olive oil
1 red onion, halved and
* sliced*
2 cloves garlic, crushed
1 tablespoon ground
* turmeric*
2 tablespoons sweet
* paprika*
1/4 teaspoon ground
* cinnamon*
2 cups long-grain white
* rice*
6 oz fresh or canned
* fava beans, skins*
* removed (or use*
* frozen peas)*
6 oz green beans,
* halved*
1 small red sweet bell
* pepper, chopped*
1 teaspoon salt
1/2 cup black olives

1. Heat the stock in a saucepan until boiling. Add the saffron and remove from the heat.
2. Meanwhile, heat the oil in a large heavy-based skillet, then add the onion, garlic, turmeric, paprika, cinnamon and rice. Stir over moderately high heat until the rice is well coated in the spice mixture.
3. Add the hot stock mixture, fava beans, green beans, red pepper and salt. Bring to a boil, then reduce the heat to moderate and simmer for 20 minutes, or until the rice is tender, stirring once. Mix in the olives, season generously with salt and pepper and serve immediately.

NUTRITION PER SERVE (6)
Protein 8 g; Fat 8 g; Carbohydrate 60 g; Dietary Fiber 6 g; Cholesterol 0 mg; 340 calories

Fragrant Paella

Stir-fried Lentils with Spinach

*Ready to eat in
25 minutes
Serves 2*

*1 cup red lentils
1 tablespoon oil
2 cloves garlic,
  crushed
1/2 teaspoon ground
  cumin
1/2 teaspoon ground
  turmeric
1/2 teaspoon sweet
  paprika
1 lb young spinach,
  stems trimmed
1/4 cup chopped
  cilantro, and extra, to
  serve
1/4 cup chopped fresh
  parsley, and extra, to
  serve
1/3 cup plain yogurt*

1. Place the lentils in a saucepan with 2 cups hot water and a generous pinch of salt. Cover partially, bring to a boil, then reduce the heat and simmer for 15 minutes, or until the lentils are tender. Drain well.
2. In a large skillet, heat the oil. Add the garlic, cumin, turmeric and paprika and stir for 2 minutes, then add the spinach.
3. When the spinach wilts, add the drained lentils, cilantro and parsley, and stir-fry until the lentils are heated through. Season with salt and freshly ground black pepper. To serve, top with the yogurt and garnish with the extra cilantro and parsley.

NUTRITION PER SERVE
*Protein 40 g; Fat 15 g;
Carbohydrate 50 g; Dietary
Fiber 35 g; Cholesterol
7 mg; 490 calories*

Note: Serve this dish with pappadams or steamed rice.

Mexican-style Pancakes

*Ready to eat in
25 minutes
Serves 4*

*1 onion, shredded
1 potato, shredded
2 zucchini,
  shredded
1 carrot, shredded
2 cloves garlic,
  crushed
1/4 cup chopped
  cilantro
1/2 cup all-purpose
  flour
3 eggs, lightly
  beaten
1/3 cup oil
sour cream and tomato
  salsa, to serve*

1. Place the shredded onion, potato, zucchini and carrot on a paper towel and squeeze out the excess moisture. Put the shredded vegetables in a bowl and stir in the garlic and cilantro. Sprinkle with the flour and stir until combined. Mix in the eggs and season well with salt and pepper.
2. Heat the oil in a large skillet. Drop half the mixture into the pan and spread out to the edges. Cook for 4–5 minutes, or until the pancake is set and golden underneath, then turn over and cook the other side. Remove and drain on paper towels. Repeat with the remaining pancake mixture.
3. Cut the pancakes into wedges and serve topped with the sour cream and tomato salsa, and a tossed green salad.

NUTRITION PER SERVE
*Protein 7.5 g; Fat 28 g;
Carbohydrate 15 g; Dietary
Fiber 3 g; Cholesterol
135 mg; 337 calories*

Note: The pancakes can be made into smaller individual pancakes and served in stacks, topped with the sour cream and either home-made or bottled tomato salsa.

*Stir-fried Lentils with Spinach (top)
and Mexican-style Pancakes*

Polenta Cake with Chili Bean Salsa

*Ready to eat in
30 minutes*
Serves 6

1 cup self-rising flour
1 teaspoon salt
1 1/2 cups fine instant
  polenta
1 cup shredded
  Cheddar
1 teaspoon cumin seeds
1 1/4 cups buttermilk
3 eggs, lightly beaten
1/4 cup butter, melted

Chili Bean Salsa
1 tablespoon oil
1 red onion, sliced
4 cloves garlic, crushed
2 teaspoons ground
  cumin
1 teaspoon chili powder
16 oz can red kidney
  beans, rinsed and
  drained
16 oz can crushed
  tomatoes
1 red sweet bell pepper,
  diced
1/2 cup chopped
  cilantro leaves

1. Preheat the oven
to 400°F. Grease a
12 x 10 inch jelly roll
pan and line it with
parchment paper,
extending over 2 sides.
2. To make the polenta
cake, sift the flour and
salt into a bowl. Stir in
the polenta, cheese and
cumin seeds and make
a well in the center.

Combine the liquid
ingredients and stir
in until just combined.
Spread into the pan and
bake for 20 minutes.
3. Meanwhile, make the
salsa. Heat the oil in a
saucepan and cook the
onion for 3–4 minutes,
or until soft. Add the
garlic and spices and
cook for 1 minute. Add
the beans, tomatoes and
red pepper; bring to a
boil, then simmer for
10 minutes. Season well
and stir in the cilantro.
4. Serve the polenta
immediately, cut into
wedges and topped
with the salsa.

NUTRITION PER SERVE
*Protein 20 g; Fat 25 g;
Carbohydrate 25 g; Dietary
Fiber 8 g; Cholesterol
140 mg; 530 calories*

Tofu Kebabs with Herbed Couscous

*Ready to eat in
30 minutes*
Serves 4

Dressing
2 tablespoons olive
  oil
1/4 cup sweet chili
  sauce
2 tablespoons soy sauce
2 cloves garlic,
  crushed
1 teaspoon grated fresh
  ginger

6 oz firm tofu, cubed
5 oz button
  mushrooms, halved
1 red sweet bell pepper,
  cubed
1 yellow sweet bell
  pepper, cubed
2 zucchini, thickly
  sliced
1 lb couscous
2 cups boiling vegetable
  stock
2 tablespoons butter
1/2 cup chopped fresh
  herbs

1. Preheat the broiler to
high. Mix together the
dressing ingredients.
2. Thread the tofu and
vegetables alternately
tonto 12 large skewers.
Brush with the dressing.
Turning and basting,
broil for 10 minutes.
3. Put the couscous in a
bowl. Add the stock.
Stand for 2–3 minutes,
then add the butter and
herbs and fluff up the
grains with a fork. Serve
the kebabs on a bed of
couscous, drizzled with
the remaining dressing.

NUTRITION PER SERVE
*Protein 15 g; Fat 20 g;
Carbohydrate 75 g; Dietary
Fiber 4 g; Cholesterol
20 mg; 525 calories*

Note: Pre-soak wooden
skewers for 30 minutes
before using to prevent
them from burning.

---

*Polenta Cake with Chili Bean Salsa (top)
and Tofu Kebabs with Herbed Couscous*

Tagliatelle with Spinach and Peas

*Ready to eat in
25 minutes
Serves 4*

1 lb fresh tagliatelle or
   fettuccine
2¹/2 tablespoons
   butter
2 leeks, thinly sliced
¹/4 teaspoon ground
   nutmeg
1 cup frozen baby peas
2 tablespoons dry
   white wine
1 cup whipping
   cream
¹/4 cup grated
   Parmesan
3 oz young spinach,
   washed and trimmed

1. Cook the pasta in a large saucepan of boiling water for 3–5 minutes, or until just tender. Drain, set aside and keep warm.
2. Meanwhile, heat the butter in a saucepan. Add the leeks and nutmeg; cover and cook over low heat for 5 minutes, shaking the pan occasionally. Add the peas and wine, then cook, covered, for 3 minutes.
3. Add the cream and season with salt and freshly ground black pepper. Bring to a boil, and cook for about 3 minutes. Stir in the Parmesan and spinach; cover and remove from the heat. Divide the pasta among serving bowls and spoon the sauce on top.

NUTRITION PER SERVE
Protein 20 g; Fat 40 g; Carbohydrate 95 g; Dietary Fiber 10 g; Cholesterol 115 mg; 815 calories

Warm Tomato and Asparagus Salad

*Ready to eat in
25 minutes
Serves 4–6*

Dressing
¹/3 cup extra virgin
   olive oil
2 tablespoons balsamic
   vinegar
1 teaspoon coarse-grain
   mustard
¹/2 teaspoon sugar

1 lb plum tomatoes,
   halved
1 tablespoon olive
   oil
1 tablespoon soft
   brown sugar
6 oz fresh asparagus,
   trimmed
8 oz canned lima or
   butter beans, drained
6 oz mixed salad
   leaves
2 tablespoons fresh
   oregano

1. Combine all the dressing ingredients and season with salt and freshly ground black pepper. Mix well and set aside.
2. Preheat the broiler to high. Put the tomatoes cut-side-up on a broiler tray; brush with oil and sprinkle with the sugar and a little salt and pepper. Make sure the tray is at least 1¹/4 inches from the heat and broil the tomatoes, turning once, for 7 minutes, or until brown on top and just softened. Turn off the heat and keep the tomatoes warm.
3. Meanwhile, bring some water to a boil in a saucepan. Add the asparagus and cook over very high heat for 1–2 minutes, or until it is bright green and just tender. Drain.
4. Put the lima beans in a bowl, add three quarters of the dressing and toss to combine.
5. Arrange the salad leaves, tomatoes and asparagus on serving plates. Spoon the bean mixture on top, scatter with oregano and drizzle with the remaining dressing to serve.

NUTRITION PER SERVE (6)
Protein 4.5 g; Fat 15 g; Carbohydrate 10 g; Dietary Fiber 4.5 g; Cholesterol 0 mg; 205 calories

*Tagliatelle with Spinach and Peas (top)
and Warm Tomato and Asparagus Salad*

Delicious Dips and Spreads

Artichoke and Tofu Purée

Drain a 13 oz can of artichoke hearts. Place in a food processor with 2 chopped garlic cloves, 5 oz drained silken tofu, 2 tablespoons lemon juice and 1/2 teaspoon finely grated lemon rind. Process until combined.

Serve with vegetable crudités or crackers. *Ready to eat in 12 minutes. Serves 4*

NUTRITION PER SERVE
Protein 5.5 g; Fat 2 g; Carbohydrate 2 g; Dietary Fiber 1 g; Cholesterol 0 mg; 50 calories

Olive and Chickpea Dip

Drain and rinse 10 oz canned chickpeas and place in a food processor with 2/3 cup pitted Kalamata olives, about 1/2 teaspoon chopped red chile and 2 crushed garlic cloves. Process until coarsely chopped, then slowly add 1/4 cup olive oil while the motor is still running. Serve with toasted pita bread. *Ready to eat in 12 minutes. Serves 6*

NUTRITION PER SERVE
Protein 3.5 g; Fat 10 g; Carbohydrate 7.5 g; Dietary Fiber 3 g; Cholesterol 0 mg; 145 calories

From left to right: Artichoke and Tofu Purée; Olive and Chickpea Dip; Cheese and Walnut Spread; Eggplant Dip; Bean Pureé with Fresh Herbs

Cheese and Walnut Spread

Beat 6 oz ricotta, 4 oz softened blue cheese and 1/2 cup finely chopped toasted walnuts until light, creamy and well combined. Season and serve with slices of toasted French bread.
Ready to eat in 10 minutes. Serves 6

NUTRITION PER SERVE
Protein 8.5 g; Fat 15 g; Carbohydrate 0.5 g; Dietary Fiber 0.5 g; Cholesterol 35 mg; 175 calories

Eggplant Dip

Preheat the oven to 425°F. Roast 2 small eggplants and 1 red sweet bell pepper for 20 minutes, or until tender and wrinkled. Cool briefly. Halve the eggplants and scoop the flesh into a food processor. Add the peeled red pepper flesh to the eggplant with 1 chopped garlic clove and 1 tablespoon lemon juice. Process until smooth; season. Serve with rice crackers.
Ready to eat in 25 minutes. Serves 4

NUTRITION PER SERVE
Protein 1.5 g; Fat 0 g; Carbohydrate 4 g; Dietary Fiber 3 g; Cholesterol 0 mg; 25 calories

Bean Purée with Fresh Herbs

Rinse and drain a 10 oz can of cannellini beans. Place in a food processor with 2 chopped garlic cloves. 1 tablespoon lemon juice and 1/2 teaspoon each chopped fresh rosemary and parsley. Process until combined. With the motor running, add 1/4 cup olive oil and process to a thick purée. Serve with crusty bread.
Ready to eat in 15 minutes. Serves 4

NUTRITION PER SERVE
Protein 6 g; Fat 15 g; Carbohydrate 15 g; Dietary Fiber 1 g; Cholesterol 0 mg; 215 calories

Tangy Noodle Salad

Ready to eat in 20 minutes
Serves 4

Dressing
1 tablespoon sesame oil
2 teaspoons brown sugar
1/4 cup lime juice
1 tablespoon rice vinegar
2 tablespoons sliced lemon grass, white part only (see Note)

3 oz cellophane (bean thread) noodles
2 short, thin cucumbers
2 carrots, shredded
1 cup bean sprouts
1 red onion, thinly sliced
1/2 cup chopped cilantro
1 cup chopped fresh mint
1/4 cup chopped roasted unsalted peanuts
romaine lettuce, to serve

1. Place the dressing ingredients in a large bowl and whisk well with a fork. Set aside.
2. Put the noodles in a large heatproof bowl. Cover with boiling water and soak for 5 minutes. Drain, then cut into short lengths using a pair of scissors. Add to the dressing and toss well.

3. Using a vegetable peeler, peel long ribbons from the cucumbers. Add to the noodles with the carrot, sprouts, onion, cilantro, mint and most of the peanuts. Mix gently. Arrange the lettuce on a large platter. Top with the noodles and sprinkle with the remaining peanuts.

NUTRITION PER SERVE
Protein 5.5 g; Fat 10 g; Carbohydrate 30 g; Dietary Fiber 3.5 g; Cholesterol 0 mg; 230 calories

Note: Lemon grass is available in Asian (Thai) food markets.

Roast Vegie Salad

Ready to eat in 30 minutes
Serves 4

1 lb new potatoes, thickly sliced
12 oz butternut squash, peeled and cut into 1/2 inch cubes
3 slender eggplants, sliced
2 tablespoons olive oil
8 oz cherry tomatoes
6 oz button mushrooms, halved
romaine lettuce, to serve
6 oz soy cheese, cubed (see Note)
1/2 cup pumpkin seeds (pepitas)

Dressing
2 tablespoons extra virgin olive oil
2 tablespoons balsamic vinegar
1 teaspoon crushed garlic

1. Preheat the oven to 500°F. Put the potatoes, squash and eggplant in a large roasting pan and drizzle with the oil. Season, toss well and roast for 10 minutes.
2. Mix in the tomatoes and mushrooms and roast for 10 minutes longer. Remove from the oven. Stir in the combined dressing ingredients.
3. Arrange some lettuce leaves around a large dish; sprinkle with some shredded lettuce. Spoon on the vegetables, then sprinkle with the cheese and pumpkin seeds.

NUTRITION PER SERVE
Protein 10 g; Fat 15 g; Carbohydrate 30 g; Dietary Fiber 10 g; Cholesterol 0 mg; 285 calories

Note: Soy cheese is sold in health food shops and some supermarkets. You could use vegetarian cheese instead, or a strong-flavored cheese such as blue cheese, Camembert or Brie.

Tangy Noodle Salad (top) and Roast Vegie Salad

Hot Tofu Salad

*Ready to eat in
 25 minutes
Serves 4*

*1/4 cup sweet chili
 sauce
1 teaspoon crushed
 garlic
1 teaspoon grated fresh
 ginger
2 tablespoons soy
 sauce
1 lb firm tofu, cut into
 1/2 inch cubes
2 tablespoons oil
2 carrots, sliced
2 zucchini, sliced
6 green onions,
 sliced
3 oz sugar snap peas,
 trimmed*

1. Place the sweet chili
sauce, garlic, ginger
and soy sauce in a
bowl. Add the tofu.
Cover and marinate for
10 minutes.
2. Drain the tofu,
reserving the marinade.
Heat half the oil in a
large skillet. Add the
tofu and cook over
high heat for about
4 minutes, or until it is
nicely browned all over,
turning often. Remove
and set aside.
3. Heat the remaining
oil. Add the vegetables
and toss over high heat
for 2–3 minutes. Add

the tofu and reserved
marinade. Bring to a
boil, stirring gently to
combine the mixture.
Remove from the heat
and serve at once.

NUTRITION PER SERVE
*Protein 15 g; Fat 15 g;
Carbohydrate 25 g; Dietary
Fiber 5.5 g; Cholesterol
0 mg; 305 calories*

Stuffed Mushrooms

*Ready to eat in
 30 minutes
Serves 4*

*4 large open, flat
 mushrooms
2 tablespoons
 butter
1 leek, sliced
2–4 cloves garlic,
 crushed
2 teaspoons cumin
 seeds
1 teaspoon ground
 coriander
1/4–1/2 teaspoon chili
 powder
2 tomatoes,
 chopped
2 cups mixed frozen
 vegetables
1/2 cup cooked white
 rice
1/3 cup shredded
 Cheddar
1/4 cup grated
 Parmesan
1/4 cup cashew nuts,
 chopped*

1. Preheat the oven to
400°F. Wipe the
mushrooms clean using
a paper towel. Remove
the stems and chop
them finely.
2. Meanwhile, melt the
butter in a saucepan.
Add the chopped
mushroom stems and
leek and cook for
2–3 minutes, or until
soft. Mix in the garlic,
cumin seeds, ground
coriander and chili
powder and cook for
1 minute, or until the
mixture is fragrant.
3. Stir in the tomatoes
and frozen vegetables.
Bring to a boil, reduce
the heat and simmer for
5 minutes. Stir in the
rice and season well
with salt and freshly
ground black pepper.
4. Spoon the mixture
into the mushroom
caps, sprinkle with the
Cheddar and Parmesan,
transfer to the oven and
bake for 15 minutes, or
until the cheese has
melted. Scatter with
the chopped cashew
nuts to serve.

NUTRITION PER SERVE
*Protein 10 g; Fat 15 g;
Carbohydrate 15 g; Dietary
Fiber 7 g; Cholesterol
35 mg; 250 calories*

Note: Any vegetables
can be used instead of
frozen vegetables. We
used carrots, peas, corn
and turnip.

*Hot Tofu Salad (top)
and Stuffed Mushrooms*

17

Butter Bean Korma Curry

*Ready to eat in
  30 minutes*
Serves 4

1 tablespoon oil
1 large onion, sliced
2 cloves garlic, crushed
*4 teaspoons garam
  masala*
*1 teaspoon ground
  coriander*
*1 teaspoon ground
  cumin*
1 teaspoon chili powder
*1/4 teaspoon ground
  turmeric*
*14 oz can unsweetened
  coconut cream*
*1 lb button
  mushrooms, halved*
*1/2 cup finely ground
  almonds (almond
  meal)*
*2 tablespoons tomato
  paste*
*2 x 10 oz cans butter or
  lima beans, drained*
*1 red sweet bell pepper,
  sliced*
2 teaspoons lemon juice
*1/4 cup chopped
  cilantro*

1. Heat the oil in a large saucepan and fry the onion and garlic until golden. Add the ground spices; cook for 1–2 minutes, or until fragrant.
2. Add the coconut cream and bring to a boil. Reduce the heat and add the mushrooms, ground almonds, tomato paste and 1 cup water. Cover and bring to a boil. Reduce the heat and simmer, uncovered, for 10 minutes, stirring occasionally.
3. Add the beans and red pepper and cook for 5 minutes, or until the sauce has thickened. Stir in the lemon juice and cilantro. Serve with steamed rice and plain yogurt.

NUTRITION PER SERVE
*Protein 15 g; Fat 40 g;
Carbohydrate 15 g; Dietary
Fiber 10 g; Cholesterol
0 mg; 480 calories*

Note: To reduce the cooking time, use very small mushrooms.

Watercress Soufflé Omelet

*Ready to eat in
  20 minutes*
Serves 2

*8 oz watercress, stems
  trimmed*
1/4 cup butter
1 small onion, shredded
pinch of ground nutmeg
4 eggs, separated
1/4 cup sour cream
*1/4 cup shredded
  Cheddar*

1. Finely chop the watercress. Melt 4 teaspoons of the butter in a skillet, add the watercress, onion and nutmeg and fry gently for 2–3 minutes, or until the watercress is wilted and tender. Keep warm in the pan.
2. Beat the egg yolks and sour cream with some salt and freshly ground pepper until well combined.
3. Using an electric mixer, beat the egg whites in a bowl until soft peaks form. Gently fold into the egg-yolk mixture in 2 batches.
4. Preheat the broiler to high. Heat the rest of the butter in a large ovenproof skillet, then spoon in the egg mixture. When the underneath has set and the omelet is half cooked, spoon the watercress mixture over one half and sprinkle with the cheese. Broil until set and puffed, then slide onto a plate and fold over to encase the filling. Cut in half and serve at once.

NUTRITION PER SERVE
*Protein 20 g; Fat 50 g;
Carbohydrate 5 g; Dietary
Fiber 5.5 g; Cholesterol
485 mg; 565 calories*

Note: This is also good with Swiss cheese.

*Butter Bean Korma Curry (top)
with Watercress Soufflé Omelet*

Speedy Soups

Mixed-bean Soup with Croutons

Heat 1 tablespoon oil in a large saucepan. Add a chopped onion and 2 crushed garlic cloves. Cook for 3 minutes. Add 1/2 teaspoon chili powder, 2 teaspoons ground coriander and 1 tablespoon ground cumin; fry for 1 minute.

Add 1 tablespoon tomato paste, two 16 oz cans chopped tomatoes and 2 cups vegetable stock. Bring to a boil, reduce the heat and simmer for 10 minutes. Add 1 1/2 lb canned, drained and rinsed mixed beans, such as cannellini, lima, red kidney and chickpeas. Simmer for 5 minutes, then add 2 tablespoons shredded fresh basil and season well. Meanwhile, make

the croutons: brush 2 lavosh (soft Armenian cracker bread) with 1 tablespoon olive oil, sprinkle with seasoned pepper and cut into 3/4 inch wide strips. Bake in a 350°F oven for 5 minutes, or until crisp and golden. *Ready to eat in 25 minutes. Serves 6–8*

NUTRITION PER SERVE (8)
Protein 8 g; Fat 4 g; Carbohydrate 20 g; Dietary Fiber 8 g; Cholesterol 0 mg; 150 calories

From left to right: Mixed-bean Soup with Croutons; Curried Lentil Soup; Vegetarian Pho

Curried Lentil Soup

Heat 2 tablespoons oil in a large saucepan and add 1 finely chopped onion. Cook over medium heat for 3 minutes, or until soft. Add a teaspoon crushed garlic and cook until golden, then add 2–3 tablespoons mild curry paste and cook until fragrant. Add 1 cup red lentils and 4 cups vegetable stock; simmer for 10–15 minutes. Stir in 2 cups mixed frozen vegetables and 8 oz unthawed frozen spinach and cook for 5 minutes, or until the vegetables are tender. Serve with yogurt and cashew nuts.
Ready to eat in 30 minutes. Serves 4

NUTRITION PER SERVE
Protein 20 g; Fat 20 g; Carbohydrate 30 g; Dietary Fiber 15 g; Cholesterol 0 mg; 560 calories

Vegetarian Pho

In a large saucepan, bring 5 cups vegetable stock to a simmer. Add 3 oz fresh Chinese egg noodles (Hokkien noodles), a tablespoon grated fresh ginger and 5 oz sliced deep-fried bean curd. Simmer for 5 minutes. Add 2 oz torn young spinach leaves and 2 thinly sliced green onions. Simmer for 3 minutes. Season and add 1 tablespoon lime juice. Lift the noodles into bowls and top with 1 cup bean sprouts. Ladle in the soup. Sprinkle with a thinly sliced red chile and 1/2 cup each mint and cilantro leaves.
Ready to eat in 25 minutes. Serves 4

NUTRITION PER SERVE
Protein 7 g; Fat 15 g; Carbohydrate 20 g; Dietary Fiber 2 g; Cholesterol 0 mg; 260 calories

Fresh Herb Falafel

*Ready to eat in
30 minutes*
Serves 4

Falafel
*1 small onion,
halved*
1 cup fresh parsley
1/4 cup cilantro
*10 oz can chickpeas or
cannellini beans,
drained and rinsed*
*1 teaspoon ground
cumin*
*1 teaspoon ground
coriander*

oil, for pan-frying
*1/2 cup sesame
seeds*
*1 1/2 cups bottled
tomato pasta sauce*
*1 teaspoon soft brown
sugar*
*2 teaspoons balsamic
vinegar*
*6 oz mixed lettuce
leaves*

1. To make the falafel,
finely chop the onion,
parsley and cilantro in
a food processor. Add
the chickpeas, cumin
and coriander. Process
for 15 seconds, or until
well combined.
2. Heat the oil in a
skillet. Shape the falafel
into 8 patties and roll
in the sesame seeds.

Cook the falafel in
batches over medium
heat for 2 minutes on
each side, or until dark
gold and cooked
through. Drain on
paper towels
3. Meanwhile, bring
the pasta sauce, sugar
and vinegar to a boil.
Reduce the heat and
simmer for 3 minutes.
4. Place the lettuce on
serving plates, arrange
the falafel on top, and
top with the sauce.

NUTRITION PER SERVE
*Protein 10 g; Fat 25 g;
Carbohydrate 15 g; Dietary
Fiber 10 g; Cholesterol
0 mg; 340 calories*

Wild Mushroom Tarts

*Ready to eat in
30 minutes*
Serves 4

4 sheets phyllo pastry
1/4 cup butter, melted
2 tablespoons olive oil
*4 cloves garlic,
crushed*
*6 green onions,
sliced*
*14 oz mixed wild
mushrooms, such as
cèpe, shiitake, enoki,
oyster*
*2 tablespoons chopped
fresh parsley, and
extra, to serve*
1/3 cup plain yogurt

1. Preheat the oven to
350°F. Brush eight
1/2 cup muffin cups
with melted butter.
Lay the phyllo sheets
on top of each other,
and cut into six even
rectangles. Brush each
phyllo sheet with the
melted butter, and pile
6 sheets, overlapping
at angles, into each
muffin cup. Bake for
5–10 minutes, or until
the pastry is golden
and crisp.
2. Heat the oil in a
large skillet. Add the
garlic and green onions
and cook over medium
heat for 2–3 minutes.
Add the mushrooms,
slicing any that are
large, then cook for
5 minutes, or until
they are soft and
tender. Season and stir
in the parsley.
3. Carefully spoon the
mushroom mixture
into the pastry cases.
Dot with the yogurt
and sprinkle with the
extra parsley. Serve
with a salad.

NUTRITION PER SERVE
*Protein 7 g; Fat 25 g;
Carbohydrate 10 g; Dietary
Fiber 4 g; Cholesterol
40 mg; 285 calories*

Variation: For special
occasions, you can use
a cheese such as
peppered Brie on the
warm tarts instead of
the yogurt.

*Fresh Herb Falafel (top)
and Wild Mushroom Tarts*

Couscous Salad

*Ready to eat in
25 minutes
Serves 4*

2 1/2 cups small broccoli
  florets
2 zucchini, sliced
2 carrots, sliced
3/4 cup halved green
  beans
1 cup frozen corn
  kernels, thawed
1 3/4 cups couscous
2 cups boiling vegetable
  stock
2 tablespoons
  butter
1/2 cup chopped fresh
  flat-leaf parsley
1/4 cup extra virgin
  olive oil
2 tablespoons lemon
  juice
2 tablespoons chopped
  preserved lemon rind
  (see Note)

1. Microwave, steam or
boil the vegetables until
tender. Set aside.
2. Put the couscous in a
large bowl and add the
hot stock. Cover with
foil for 3–4 minutes.
Remove the foil and
mix in the butter using
a fork. Mix in the
vegetables and parsley.
3. Place the remaining
ingredients in a screw-
top jar with some salt
and pepper. Shake well,
then pour over the
salad. Toss the salad
well and serve.

NUTRITION PER SERVE
*Protein 10 g; Fat 20 g;
Carbohydrate 60 g; Dietary
Fiber 7.5 g; Cholesterol
20 mg; 475 calories*

Note: Preserved lemon
is often sold in specialty
food shops. If you can't
find any, you could use
1 teaspoon grated
lemon rind instead.

Haloumi with Tomato, Olives and Capers

*Ready to eat in
25 minutes
Serves 4*

1/2 cup olive oil
2 tablespoons capers,
  drained and dried
1 lb haloumi cheese
1/4 cup all-purpose
  flour
1 1/2 cups young
  spinach leaves
1/3 cup sliced black
  olives
1 large ripe tomato,
  diced
2 tablespoons balsamic
  vinegar
fresh oregano sprigs, to
  garnish

1. Heat 1 tablespoon
of the oil in a small
saucepan over medium
heat. Add the capers
and gently cook for
5 minutes, or until

crisp, stirring
occasionally. Drain on
paper towels.
2. Meanwhile, cut the
haloumi into 8 slices
and pat dry with paper
towels. Lightly coat in
the flour.
3. In a large skillet,
heat 2 tablespoons of
the oil over medium
heat. Add half the
cheese slices and cook
for 1–1 1/2 minutes a
side, or until golden
brown. Remove and
drain on paper towels.
Repeat with the
remaining cheese.
4. Arrange the spinach
leaves on a platter.
Top with the pan-
fried cheese slices,
overlapping them a
little. Scatter with the
olives, tomato, capers
and some black pepper.
Drizzle with the vinegar
and remaining olive oil.
Garnish with the
oregano sprigs and
serve immediately.

NUTRITION PER SERVE
*Protein 25 g; Fat 45 g;
Carbohydrate 6 g; Dietary
Fiber 1.5 g; Cholesterol
40 mg; 500 calories*

Note: Haloumi is a
salty, soft-textured
Greek cheese, sold in
many delicatessens. It
should be used within
2 days of purchase.

*Couscous Salad (top)
and Haloumi with Tomato, Olives and Capers*

Stir-fried Greens with Tofu Tempeh

Ready to eat in
  25 minutes
Serves 4

2 tablespoons peanut
  oil
8 oz tofu tempeh, cut
  into large cubes
1 tablespoon finely
  chopped fresh ginger
2 cloves garlic,
  crushed
1–2 chopped small red
  chiles, or to taste
4 green onions,
  chopped
2 celery stalks,
  sliced
3 oz baby green beans,
  trimmed
1 teaspoon sugar
1 teaspoon salt
2 1/2 cups small broccoli
  florets
6 oz fresh asparagus, cut
  into 1 1/2 inch pieces
1 tablespoon soy
  sauce
1 1/2 cups young
  spinach leaves

1. Heat half the oil in a
wok or skillet over high
heat until hot. Add the
tofu tempeh and stir-fry
for 3 minutes, or until
golden and slightly
crisp. Drain on paper
towels and set aside,
covered with paper
towels to keep warm.
2. Heat the remaining
oil in the wok. Add the
ginger, garlic, chile and
green onions and stir-
fry for 15 seconds. Add
the celery, beans, sugar
and salt, and stir-fry for
1 minute.
3. Add 2 tablespoons
water; cover and cook
for 1 minute. Add the
broccoli florets and
asparagus, toss well,
and cook, covered, for
2 minutes.
4. Stir in the soy sauce,
spinach leaves and
tofu tempeh and
serve immediately.

NUTRITION PER SERVE
*Protein 9 g; Fat 12 g;
Carbohydrate 5 g; Dietary
Fiber 4 g; Cholesterol
0 mg; 165 calories*

Notes: Tofu tempeh
is a fermented soy
bean product, sold
in vacuum packs at
good supermarkets
and health food
stores. In this recipe,
tempeh burgers or
deep-fried tofu may be
used instead.
  Baby green beans
are used in this recipe
to reduce the cooking
time. If they are not
available, use regular
beans instead: simply
trim them and cut them
in half.

Burrito Pinwheels

Ready to eat in
  25 minutes
Serves 2–3

3 red sweet bell peppers
olive oil, for cooking
4 flour tortillas
1 cup hummus
  (chickpea dip)
1 cup chopped fresh
  parsley

1. Preheat the broiler to
high. Cut the red
peppers into eighths,
discarding the seeds
and white membrane,
and brush all over with
a little oil. Broil both
sides until softened.
Allow to cool.
2. Spread each tortilla
with some of the
hummus, then top with
some pepper strips and
sprinkle with the
parsley. Season with
salt and pepper. Roll
up firmly, slice into
1 1/2 inch rounds and
serve with a salad or
as a light meal.

NUTRITION PER SERVE (3)
*Protein 20 g; Fat 35 g;
Carbohydrate 40 g; Dietary
Fiber 10 g; Cholesterol
0 mg; 475 calories*

Note: Tortillas are
Mexican flat breads,
available in most
supermarkets. Lavosh
(soft Armenian
cracker bread) may
also be used.

*Stir-fried Greens with Tofu Tempeh (top)
and Burrito Pinwheels*

Brilliant Bruschettas

Bruschetta Bread

Toast 12 slices of a crusty Italian bread loaf. While still hot, rub with a cut clove of garlic, brush with olive oil and serve with your choice of topping.
Serves 6

NUTRITION PER SERVE
Protein 5 g; Fat 10 g; Carbohydrate 25 g; Dietary Fiber 2 g; Cholesterol 0 mg; 220 calories

Zesty Zucchini Salsa

Finely chop 3 zucchini, 2 tomatoes and 1 small red onion; mix well. Stir in 1 teaspoon grated lime rind, 2 tablespoons lime juice and about 2 tablespoons of chopped cilantro.
Ready to eat in 15 minutes. Serves 6

NUTRITION PER SERVE
Protein 1 g; Fat 0 g; Carbohydrate 3 g; Dietary Fiber 1.5 g; Cholesterol 0 mg; 20 calories

Roast Vegie Topping

Preheat the oven to 475°F. Dice 2 tomatoes, 2 zucchini, 1 yellow sweet bell pepper and 1 small eggplant. Put in a roasting pan. Season well with salt and pepper and drizzle with 1 tablespoon balsamic vinegar. Roast for 15 minutes, stirring occasionally, then stir in 1/4 cup chopped fresh parsley.
Ready to eat in 30 minutes. Serves 6

NUTRITION PER SERVE
Protein 2 g; Fat 0 g; Carbohydrate 5 g; Dietary Fiber 2.5 g; Cholesterol 0 mg; 30 calories

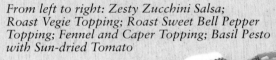

From left to right: Zesty Zucchini Salsa; Roast Vegie Topping; Roast Sweet Bell Pepper Topping; Fennel and Caper Topping; Basil Pesto with Sun-dried Tomato

Roast Sweet Bell Pepper Topping

Preheat the broiler to high. Broil a large red, a green and a yellow sweet bell pepper until black. Cool, then peel away the skin and thinly slice the flesh. Mix in 2 tablespoons toasted sesame seeds, 2/3 cup crumbled feta or goat's cheese and 1 teaspoon sesame oil.
Ready to eat in 30 minutes. Serves 6

NUTRITION PER SERVE
Protein 6 g; Fat 8.5 g; Carbohydrate 3 g; Dietary Fiber 2 g; Cholesterol 10 mg; 110 calories

Fennel and Caper Topping

Shred a small bulb fresh fennel. Add 1 tablespoon chopped capers, 2/3 cup chopped fresh parsley, 1/4 cup lemon juice, 1 teaspoon grated lemon rind, 2 tablespoons chopped pitted green olives and 1 tablespoon olive oil.
Ready to eat in 20 minutes. Serves 6

NUTRITION PER SERVE
Protein 0 g; Fat 3 g; Carbohydrate 0.5 g; Dietary Fiber 0.5 g; Cholesterol 0 mg; 45 calories

Basil Pesto with Sun-dried Tomato

In a food processor, finely chop 1 crushed garlic clove, 1/4 cup toasted pine nuts, 2 cups fresh basil leaves and 1/2 cup grated Parmesan. With the motor still running, gradually add 1/2 cup olive oil. Transfer to a bowl and stir in 1/2 cup sliced, drained sun-dried tomatoes in oil.
Ready to eat in 20 minutes. Serves 6

NUTRITION PER SERVE
Protein 4 g; Fat 25 g; Carbohydrate 0 g; Dietary Fiber 0 g; Cholesterol 8 mg; 260 calories

Note: Store the pesto, covered with oil, in a jar.

Roast Potato and Sweet Pepper Frittata

Ready to eat in 30 minutes
Serves 4

1 tablespoon olive oil
1–2 cloves garlic, crushed
1 small red onion, chopped
1 small red sweet bell pepper, chopped
5 large left-over roast potatoes, thickly sliced
1/4 cup chopped fresh parsley
6 eggs, lightly beaten
1/4 cup grated Parmesan

1. Heat the oil in a heavy-based, non-stick skillet measuring 10 inches across the top. Add the garlic, onion and red pepper. Cook, stirring, over moderate heat for 2–3 minutes. Add the potato slices and cook for 2–3 minutes more.
2. Stir in the parsley and spread the mixture evenly around the pan. Beat the eggs with 2 tablespoons water, pour into the pan and cook over medium heat for 15 minutes, without burning the frittata underneath.
3. Preheat the broiler to high. Sprinkle the Parmesan over the frittata and broil for a few minutes to cook the egg and lightly brown the top. Cut into wedges and serve.

NUTRITION PER SERVE
Protein 15 g; Fat 15 g; Carbohydrate 20 g; Dietary Fiber 4 g; Cholesterol 275 mg; 285 calories

Note: If you don't have left-over roast potatoes, you will need to boil, steam or microwave 1 lb potatoes.

Tomato Chili Penne

Ready to eat in 25 minutes
Serves 4–6

12 oz penne pasta
1/3 cup extra virgin olive oil
1 teaspoon chili oil (optional)
2–3 cloves garlic, crushed
1 small red chile, finely chopped
6 oz arugula leaves
14 oz can Mexican chili beans in tomato sauce
4 ripe tomatoes, finely chopped
1/2 cup small black olives

1. Bring a large saucepan of salted water to a boil. Add the pasta and cook for 8–10 minutes, or until just tender, yet still firm. Drain and keep warm.
2. Place the oils, garlic and chile in a small saucepan. Heat the mixture over very low heat for 5 minutes, taking care not to let it brown or the garlic will be bitter.
3. Meanwhile, remove the lower stalks from the arugula leaves. Wash and pat dry, then coarsely chop.
4. Place the beans, tomatoes and olives in a large serving bowl and season with freshly ground black pepper. Add the hot pasta and oil mixture. Gently toss together. Season to taste, then fold in the arugula leaves and serve at once.

NUTRITION PER SERVE (6)
Protein 10 g; Fat 15 g; Carbohydrate 55 g; Dietary Fiber 9 g; Cholesterol 0 mg; 400 calories

Note: You can use a drained 14 oz can of red kidney beans with 1/4 cup taco sauce instead of the Mexican chili beans.

Tomato Chili Penne (top) with
Roast Potato and Sweet Pepper Frittata

Three-bean Stir-fry

Ready to eat in 15 minutes
Serves 4

5 oz arugula leaves, washed
1 tablespoon oil
1 red onion, chopped
2 cloves garlic, crushed
1 tablespoon finely chopped fresh thyme
2 cups chopped green beans
10 oz can lima or butter beans, rinsed and drained
10 oz can chickpeas, rinsed and drained
2 tablespoons finely chopped fresh parsley
1/4 cup lemon juice, or to taste

1. Arrange the arugula in a large serving bowl and set aside.
2. Add the oil to a hot wok, swirling to coat the sides. Stir-fry the onion for 2 minutes. Add the garlic and stir-fry until the onion is soft. Add the thyme and stir-fry for 30 seconds.
3. Add the green beans and stir-fry for about 3 minutes, or until tender. Add the lima beans and chickpeas and stir-fry until heated through. Season with salt and pepper and spoon onto the arugula. Sprinkle with the parsley and drizzle with the lemon juice.

NUTRITION PER SERVE
Protein 9 g; Fat 7 g; Carbohydrate 15 g; Dietary Fiber 8.5 g; Cholesterol 0 mg; 165 calories

Bean Nachos with a Lime Cilantro Cream

Ready to eat in 25 minutes
Serves 4–6

1 tablespoon oil
2 onions, chopped
2–4 cloves garlic, crushed
1 tablespoon ground cumin
1 teaspoon ground coriander
14 oz can red kidney beans, drained and rinsed
16 oz can refried beans
1/2 cup bottled tomato salsa
4 oz can pimiento pieces, drained
7 oz package corn chips
1/2 cup shredded soy or vegetarian cheese
1 avocado, sliced

Lime Cilantro Cream
1/2 cup crème fraîche or sour cream
2 teaspoons grated lime rind
1 tablespoon chopped cilantro leaves

1. Heat the oil in a saucepan, add the onions and cook over medium heat for 4–5 minutes. Stir in the garlic and spices and cook for 1 minute. Stir in the beans, salsa and pimiento. Bring to a boil, then reduce the heat and simmer for 5–10 minutes.
2. Preheat the broiler to high. Put the bean mixture in a shallow baking dish. Arrange the corn chips around the edge and sprinkle with cheese. Broil for 3 minutes.
3. Mix together the lime cilantro cream ingredients. Garnish the nachos with avocado and top with the cream.

NUTRITION PER SERVE (6)
Protein 20 g; Fat 45 g; Carbohydrate 40 g; Dietary Fiber 20 g; Cholesterol 25 mg; 625 calories

Note: To make your own crème fraîche, mix 1 tablespoon buttermilk into 1/2 cup whipping cream. Cover and stand for 8–24 hours at 70°F, or until thick. Stir well, cover and refrigerate.

Three-bean Stir-fry (top) and Bean Nachos with a Lime Cilantro Cream

Lovely Light Meals

Mediterranean-style Salad

Toast crusty bread slices and brush with olive oil. Cool. Cut a large red and a yellow sweet bell pepper into large flat pieces. Broil until black and blistered. Cool, peel the skin, slice the flesh and place in a bowl with 6 oz halved cherry tomatoes, 1 cup loosely packed torn arugula, a sliced red onion and ½ cup Kalamata olives. Add ⅓ cup toasted almonds, a 10 oz can rinsed and drained lima or butter beans and 4 quartered hard-cooked eggs. Toss through 1 tablespoon balsamic vinegar and ¼ cup olive oil. Cut the bread into croutons; scatter on the salad and serve.
Ready to eat in 30 minutes. Serves 6

NUTRITION PER SERVE
Protein 10 g; Fat 30 g; Carbohydrate 15 g; Dietary Fiber 4 g; Cholesterol 135 mg; 360 calories

Tomato Tarts

Preheat the oven to 425°F. Cut 1 sheet of thawed frozen puff pastry into 4 squares. Place on an oiled baking sheet. Spread with ½ cup pesto, leaving a ½ inch border. Place 4 oz sliced goat's cheese on top and 4 small sliced tomatoes. Bake

From left to right: Mediterranean-style Salad; Tomato Tarts; Eggplant and Tofu Fritters

for 20 minutes, or until the edges are puffy and golden. Serve immediately with salad.
Ready to eat in 30 minutes. Serves 4

NUTRITION PER SERVE
Protein 15 g; Fat 25 g; Carbohydrate 30 g; Dietary Fiber 3 g; Cholesterol 35 mg; 395 calories

Eggplant and Tofu Fritters

Cut 8 oz firm tofu and 1 eggplant into $1/2$ inch slices. In a shallow bowl, beat 2 eggs and 4 teaspoons water. Spread $1/3$ cup all-purpose flour on a plate. Combine $1 1/2$ cups finely grated Parmesan, 2 tablespoons chopped fresh basil and 1 cup dry bread crumbs and spread on another plate. Coat the eggplant and tofu slices separately with the flour, shake off the excess, dip into the egg, then into the Parmesan mixture. Press on gently; shake off any excess. Meanwhile, heat $5/8$ inch oil in a skillet. Fry the eggplant and tofu slices in batches for 5 minutes a side, or until just golden. Drain on paper towels and serve with a warm tomato pasta sauce.
Ready to eat in 25 minutes. Serves 4

NUTRITION PER SERVE
Protein 25 g; Fat 30 g; Carbohydrate 25 g; Dietary Fiber 2 g; Cholesterol 125 mg; 500 calories

Spicy Wheat Pilaf

*Ready to eat in
25 minutes
Serves 4*

2 tablespoons olive
  oil
1 onion, chopped
5 oz button mushrooms,
  quartered
3/4 cup frozen peas
12 oz butternut squash,
  peeled and diced
1 1/2 cups bulghur
  (cracked wheat)
1/2 teaspoon ground
  cumin
1/2 teaspoon ground
  cardamom
1 teaspoon garam
  masala
1 tablespoon coriander
  seeds
1 1/2 teaspoons ground
  turmeric
1/2 teaspoon chili
  flakes
2 cups vegetable
  stock
1/4 cup chopped
  cilantro
1/2 cup dried currants
3/4 cup roasted unsalted
  cashew nuts

1. In a large saucepan,
heat the oil. Add the
onion, mushrooms,
peas and squash and
stir for 2 minutes over
medium heat, or until
the onion is soft. Add
the bulghur, spices and
chili flakes. Stir for
2 minutes, or until the
bulghur is coated with
the spices and the
mixture is aromatic.
2. Increase the heat to
high. Add the stock and
bring to a boil; reduce
the heat to very low
and cook, covered, for
15 minutes. Remove
from the heat and
mix in the cilantro,
currants and cashew
nuts to serve.

NUTRITION PER SERVE
*Protein 25 g; Fat 30 g;
Carbohydrate 35 g; Dietary
Fiber 20 g; Cholesterol
0 mg; 505 calories*

Sweet Potato Pie

*Ready to eat in
30 minutes
Serves 4*

1 sheet ready-rolled
  puff pastry,
  thawed
1/4 cup butter
4 green onions,
  chopped
12 oz sweet potato,
  peeled and finely
  diced
1/4 cup all-purpose
  flour
1 1/3 cups milk
8 oz cream cheese,
  chopped
4 oz young spinach,
  shredded
1 tablespoon sunflower
  seeds
1 tablespoon grated
  Parmesan

1. Preheat the oven to
425°F. Line a deep,
greased, loose-based
fluted 7 inch tart pan
with the pastry. Pierce
with a fork. Line with
parchment paper, fill
with dried beans or pie
weights and bake for
8 minutes. Remove
the paper and weights
and bake for 5 minutes,
or until brown and
crisp. Preheat the
broiler to hot.
2. Meanwhile, heat the
butter in a large
saucepan. Add the
green onions and sweet
potato and cook over
high heat for 5 minutes.
Add the flour and cook
until dry and beginning
to brown.
3. Remove from the
heat and slowly add the
milk, stirring constantly.
Return to the heat and
stir until boiled and
thickened, then add
the cream cheese and
spinach and stir until
the cheese melts.
4. Spoon the mixture
into the shell, sprinkle
with the remaining
ingredients and broil
for 1 minute, or until
nicely browned.

NUTRITION PER SERVE
*Protein 15 g; Fat 50 g;
Carbohydrate 40 g; Dietary
Fiber 5 g; Cholesterol
125 mg; 660 calories*

*Spicy Wheat Pilaf (top) and
Sweet Potato Pie*

Squash and Tofu Stir-fry

*Ready to eat in
30 minutes
Serves 4–6*

oil, for cooking
1 cup cashew nuts
10 oz firm tofu,
  cubed
1 leek, white part only,
  sliced
2 teaspoons ground
  coriander
2 teaspoons ground
  cumin
2 teaspoons mustard
  seeds
2 cloves garlic,
  crushed
2 lb butternut squash,
  peeled and cubed
3/4 cup orange juice
1 teaspoon soft brown
  sugar

1. Add 1 tablespoon oil to a very hot wok, swirling to coat the side, then stir-fry the cashews for 2 minutes, or until golden. Drain on paper towels.
2. Stir-fry the tofu for 2–3 minutes, or until golden. Drain and set aside. Stir-fry the leek for 2 minutes, or until softened. Remove and set aside.
3. Heat 1 tablespoon oil in the wok. Stir-fry the spices and garlic over moderate heat for 1–2 minutes, or until the seeds begin to pop. Add the squash and stir to coat.
4. Add the orange juice and sugar, bring to a boil, then cover and simmer rapidly for 5 minutes. Add the tofu and simmer, uncovered, for 5 minutes, or until the squash is tender. Add the leek and toss to combine. Top with the cashew nuts.

NUTRITION PER SERVE (6)
*Protein 7 g; Fat 15 g;
Carbohydrate 15 g; Dietary
Fiber 2.5 g; Cholesterol
0 mg; 205 calories*

Beet Burgers with a Yogurt-miso Dressing

*Ready to eat in
25 minutes
Serves 4*

Beet Burgers
1 carrot, shredded
1 beet, shredded
3 cloves garlic, crushed
2 teaspoons grated
  fresh ginger
1 egg, lightly beaten
2 teaspoons ground
  coriander
1 teaspoon ground
  cumin
3/4 cup dry bread
  crumbs

oil, for pan-frying
2 teaspoons yellow
  miso paste (shinshu)
3/4 cup plain
  yogurt
8 thick slices crusty
  Italian bread
1 cup snow pea or
  other fresh sprouts

1. To make the beet burgers, mix together the carrot, beet, garlic, ginger, egg, spices, and bread crumbs in a large bowl. Season with salt and pepper. Divide into 4 equal portions, then shape into patties.
2. Heat 3/4 inch of oil in a large skillet. Cook the burgers for about 6 minutes on each side, or until brown and cooked through. Drain on paper towels.
3. Meanwhile, preheat the broiler to high. Mix the miso paste into the yogurt. Broil the bread until crisp and serve the burgers in between with the yogurt and sprouts.

NUTRITION PER SERVE
*Protein 15 g; Fat 5 g;
Carbohydrate 50 g; Dietary
Fiber 5 g; Cholesterol
55 mg; 300 calories*

Note: Miso paste is sold in health food stores in a variety of flavors. Any miso paste can be used if yellow miso (shinshu) is not available.

*Squash and Tofu Stir-fry (top) and
Beet Burgers with a Yogurt-miso Dressing*

Eggs in an Instant

Mushroom Omelet

Melt 1/4 cup butter in an ovenproof skillet. Add 6 sliced green onions and 1 teaspoon crushed garlic; stir for 2 minutes over medium heat. Add 8 oz sliced mushrooms and cook for 2 minutes, or until tender. Lightly whisk 4 eggs with a tablespoon of water; season well. Pour into the pan and cook until almost set. Place under a hot broiler until set and light golden on top. *Ready to eat in 25 minutes. Serves 2*

NUTRITION PER SERVE
Protein 20 g; Fat 20 g; Carbohydrate 4 g; Dietary Fiber 4 g; Cholesterol 395 mg; 290 calories

Quick, Creamy Frittatas

Preheat the oven to 400°F. Grease 6 cups of a 12-cup (1/2 cup capacity) muffin pan. Shred 8 oz sweet potato, 1 onion and 2 zucchini. Place in a clean towel, squeeze out the moisture and spoon into the greased cups. Combine 6 lightly beaten eggs, 1/2 cup

From left to right: Mushroom Omelet; Quick, Creamy Frittatas; Egg and Watercress Salad

shredded Gruyère cheese and 3/4 cup whipping cream. Season and pour into the muffin cups. Bake for 15 minutes, or until the frittatas are cooked. Turn out and serve with a salad.
Ready to eat in 30 minutes. Makes 6

NUTRITION PER FRITTATA
Protein 10 g; Fat 35 g; Carbohydrate 10 g; Dietary Fiber 1.5 g; Cholesterol 270 mg; 390 calories

Egg and Watercress Salad

Cut 8 oz asparagus spears into thirds and add to a saucepan of boiling water. Cook until tender; drain and refresh in cold water. Trim 1 lb watercress and place in a serving dish. Top with 8 hard-cooked eggs, cut in half, and add the asparagus. Sprinkle with a sliced red onion and 8 oz

cherry tomatoes. Combine 1/2 cup whole-egg mayonnaise with 1 tablespoon white wine vinegar and 1 tablespoon coarse-grain mustard. Season. Drizzle over the salad and serve.
Ready to eat in 15 minutes. Serves 4

NUTRITION PER SERVE
Protein 20 g; Fat 20 g; Carbohydrate 10 g; Dietary Fiber 7 g; Cholesterol 420 mg; 315 calories

Tomato and Artichoke Risotto

*Ready to eat in
30 minutes
Serves 4*

*5 cups vegetable stock
2 tablespoons olive oil
2 small leeks, halved
and sliced
2 cloves garlic,
crushed
1 1/3 cups arborio rice
1/2 cup dry white wine
6 oz bottled quartered
artichoke hearts in oil,
drained
4 oz cherry tomatoes,
halved
2 tablespoons sun-dried
tomato pesto
grated Parmesan, to
serve*

1. Heat the vegetable
stock in a medium
saucepan until it is
simmering.
2. Meanwhile, heat the
oil in a large heavy-
based saucepan. Add the
leeks and stir over
medium-high heat for
2 minutes, or until soft.
Add the garlic, rice and
wine, and stir for
1 minute, or until
the wine has almost
evaporated.
3. Add the stock,
a ladleful at a time,
stirring with a wooden
spoon until absorbed,
then adding more stock
a ladleful at a time until
the rice is tender and
creamy. Stir in the
artichoke hearts and
tomatoes, season with
salt and freshly ground
black pepper, then
spoon into serving
bowls. Swirl in some
sun-dried tomato
pesto and sprinkle
with the grated
Parmesan to serve.

NUTRITION PER SERVE
*Protein 15 g; Fat 15 g;
Carbohydrate 65 g; Dietary
Fiber 5 g; Cholesterol
15 mg; 490 calories*

Ravioli with Tomato and Zucchini Sauce

*Ready to eat in
25 minutes
Serves 4*

*1 tablespoon olive oil
1 onion, finely
chopped
2 cloves garlic,
crushed
2 small red chiles, finely
chopped
2 zucchini, shredded
1 1/4 lb bottled tomato
pasta sauce
1 tablespoon tomato
paste
1 lb fresh cheese ravioli
or agnolotti
1/4 cup pecans, coarsely
chopped
2 tablespoons pumpkin
seeds (pepitas)*

1. Heat the oil in a
large saucepan. Add the
onion, garlic and chiles
and cook, stirring
occasionally, for
3 minutes, or until the
onion is soft.
2. Add the zucchini to
the pan and cook for
2 minutes. Stir in the
tomato pasta sauce
and tomato paste.
Bring to a boil, then
reduce the heat and
simmer, covered, for
10 minutes.
3. Meanwhile, add the
ravioli or agnolotti to a
large saucepan of
boiling water. Cook for
4 minutes, or until the
pasta is tender.
4. Drain the pasta and
stir it into the tomato
sauce. Serve the pasta
immediately, sprinkled
with the pecans and
pumpkin seeds.

NUTRITION PER SERVE
*Protein 15 g; Fat 30 g;
Carbohydrate 35 g; Dietary
Fiber 0 g; Cholesterol
20 mg; 465 calories*

Note: To make your
own cheese ravioli,
brush the edges of
wonton skins with
water. Place a heaped
tablespoon of ricotta
cheese on the center of
each square and top
with another skin. Press
the edges to seal.

---

*Tomato and Artichoke Risotto (top)
and Ravioli with Tomato and Zucchini Sauce*

Spicy Tomato Chickpea Stew

*Ready to eat in
25 minutes
Serves 4–6*

1 tablespoon olive oil
2 onions, sliced
6–8 cloves garlic,
   crushed
4 teaspoons ground
   cumin
2 teaspoons ground
   coriander
1 teaspoon sweet
   paprika
2 x 14 oz cans crushed
   tomatoes
16 oz can tomato
   purée
2 x 16 oz cans
   chickpeas, drained
   and rinsed
6 oz can pimiento
   pieces, drained
1 cup chopped fresh
   flat-leaf parsley

1. Heat the oil in a saucepan, stir in the onions and cook for 4–5 minutes over moderate heat, or until soft. Mix in the garlic and spices, and cook for 1–2 minutes. Stir in the crushed tomatoes, tomato purée, chickpeas and pimiento.
2. Bring to a boil, then reduce the heat and simmer for about 15 minutes. Season well with salt and freshly ground pepper, stir in the parsley, and serve with crusty bread.

NUTRITION PER SERVE (6)
Protein 30 g; Fat 10 g; Carbohydrate 65 g; Dietary Fiber 25 g; Cholesterol 0 mg; 475 calories

Thai Green Curry with Bean Curd

*Ready to eat in
30 minutes
Serves 3–4*

1 tablespoon oil
1 tablespoon green curry
   paste or 1/4 cup
   vegetarian green curry
   paste (see Note)
1 2/3 cups unsweetened
   coconut cream
10 oz deep-fried bean
   curd, cubed
10 oz butternut squash,
   peeled and cubed
5 oz green beans,
   trimmed
3 zucchini, thickly sliced
cilantro leaves, to
   garnish

1. Heat the oil in a heavy-based saucepan and fry the curry paste, stirring constantly, for a few seconds over high heat. Stir in the coconut cream, bring to a boil, then reduce the heat and simmer for 5 minutes.
2. Add the bean curd and vegetables. Cover and simmer gently for 15 minutes, or until the squash is just tender. Season to taste, then garnish with cilantro and serve with steamed jasmine rice.

NUTRITION PER SERVE (4)
Protein 10 g; Fat 50 g; Carbohydrate 10 g; Dietary Fiber 5 g; Cholesterol 0 mg; 500 calories

Note: Some curry pastes contain shrimp paste or fish sauce. To make a vegetarian green curry paste, place 1 teaspoon cumin seeds in a skillet with 2 teaspoons coriander seeds. Dry-fry for 2 minutes, or until fragrant, shaking the pan often. Grind finely in a mortar and pestle with 1/2 teaspoon black peppercorns, then purée in a blender with 4 large green chiles, a chopped onion, 5 garlic cloves, 2 stems chopped fresh lemon grass, 1 teaspoon each salt and grated lime rind, 2 teaspoons chopped fresh galangal or ginger, 1/2 cup chopped cilantro, and 1 tablespoon each lime juice and oil. Refrigerate in an airtight container for 3–4 weeks, or freeze in small portions. Makes 1 cup.

*Spicy Tomato Chickpea Stew (top)
and Thai Green Curry with Tofu*

Stir-fried Hokkien Noodles

*Ready to eat in
15 minutes
Serves 4*

*1 lb Hokkien noodles
(fresh Chinese egg
noodles), gently
separated
oil, for cooking
4 cloves garlic,
crushed
2 tablespoons sliced
fresh lemon grass,
white part only
1 teaspoon chopped red
chile
1 teaspoon grated fresh
ginger
5 oz yard-long beans,
chopped
6 oz fresh shiitake
mushrooms, halved
8 oz firm tofu, sliced
5 green onions, sliced
4 teaspoons kecap
manis (see Note)
4 teaspoons soy sauce
1 tablespoon sesame
seeds
2 tablespoons crispy-
fried onion (see Note)*

1. Place the Hokkien noodles in a heatproof bowl. Cover with boiling water and allow to stand for 2 minutes. Remove and drain well.
2. Heat 1 tablespoon oil in the wok and stir-fry the garlic, lemon grass, chile and ginger for 1 minute. Add the beans and mushrooms and stir-fry for 3 minutes. Add the tofu, green onions, kecap manis, soy sauce and sesame seeds and cook for 3 minutes. Add the warm noodles and 1 tablespoon water and stir-fry until heated through. Serve at once, sprinkled with the crispy-fried onion.

NUTRITION PER SERVE
*Protein 20 g; Fat 20 g;
Carbohydrate 55 g; Dietary
Fiber 4 g; Cholesterol
0 mg; 500 calories*

Note: Kecap manis is a thick, sweet, Indonesian soy sauce sold in Asian food stores. Honey can be used instead. Crispy-fried onion is also sold in Asian food stores.

Soba Noodle Salad

*Ready to eat in
20 minutes
Serves 4*

*8 oz soba noodles
(Japanese buckwheat
noodles)
1 carrot, sliced
2 celery stalks, sliced
1 cucumber, sliced
1/4 cup pickled ginger
1/3 cup cilantro leaves
3 eggs
oil, for cooking*

*Dressing
1 teaspoon sesame oil
2 1/2 tablespoons rice
vinegar
2 teaspoons soy sauce
4 teaspoons mirin
2 1/2 tablespoons lime
juice
2 tablespoons toasted
sesame seeds*

1. Cook the noodles in a large saucepan of boiling water for 6 minutes, or until tender. Drain and rinse well under cold water.
2. Blanch the carrot and celery for 1 minute in a pan of boiling water. Drain, plunge into cold water and drain well. Gently mix the vegetables into the noodles with the cucumber, pickled ginger and cilantro.
3. Lightly beat the eggs with 1 tablespoon of water. Heat a little oil in a skillet, add the egg and cook until set, then turn and cook the other side. Cut into shreds and toss into the salad.
4. Mix the dressing ingredients together, add to the salad and toss well to combine.

NUTRITION PER SERVE
*Protein 15 g; Fat 30 g;
Carbohydrate 50 g; Dietary
Fiber 5 g; Cholesterol
135 mg; 515 calories*

*Stir-fried Hokkien Noodles (top)
with Soba Noodle Salad*

um heat for about 3 minutes, or until soft and golden. Add the garlic, ginger and spices and cook until fragrant.

3. Add the lentils and 2 cups water and bring to a boil. Reduce the heat to a simmer and cook for 15 minutes, or until nearly all the liquid has been absorbed and the dhal is thick. Stir in the chopped mint and serve with naan bread.

NUTRITION PER SERVE (6)
Protein 4 g; Fat 6 g; Carbohydrate 6 g; Dietary Fiber 2 g; Cholesterol 15 mg; 95 calories

Crispy Cabbage Salad on Nori

Ready to eat in 25 minutes
Serves 4

Dressing
2 teaspoons sesame oil
2 tablespoons soy sauce
1/4 teaspoon Chinese five-spice powder
1 tablespoon tahini (sesame seed paste)

1/2 cup rice wine vinegar
2 teaspoons honey
1 teaspoon finely chopped fresh ginger

2 tablespoons peanut oil

8 oz firm tofu, cut into 1/4 inch slices

1 cucumber
6 oz hot mustard cress or alfalfa sprouts
1 lb 4 oz red cabbage, shredded
1 cup bean sprouts
4 green onions, thinly sliced diagonally
8 sheets nori (see Note)

1. To make the dressing, combine the sesame oil, soy sauce, five-spice powder, tahini, rice wine vinegar, honey and ginger in a small bowl. Set aside.
2. Heat the peanut oil in a large skillet. Add the tofu and cook in batches until it is crisp and golden. Drain on paper towels. Allow the tofu to cool, then cut into matchsticks.
3. Cut the cucumber in half lengthwise, then slice thinly. Place in a large bowl with the

mustard cress or alfalfa sprouts, cabbage, bean sprouts and green onions. Arrange two nori sheets on each serving plate and top with the salad.
4. Sprinkle the tofu onto the salad and drizzle with the dressing to serve.

NUTRITION PER SERVE
Protein 10 g; Fat 20 g; Carbohydrate 15 g; Dietary Fiber 9 g; Cholesterol 0 mg; 270 calories

Note: Nori are thin, crispy sheets of seaweed sold in sealed packages of 10.

Indian Dhal (top) and Crispy Cabbage Salad on Nori

Chickpeas and Couscous with Harissa

Ready to eat in 20 minutes
Serves 4–6

Harissa Dressing
1/3 cup olive oil
2 tablespoons lime or lemon juice
2 teaspoons harissa
1 small clove garlic, crushed

1/2 cup instant couscous
2 x 16 oz cans chickpeas, drained and rinsed
4 green onions, finely chopped
12 cherry tomatoes, halved
1/3 cup chopped fresh mint
1/3 cup chopped cilantro

1. To make the harissa dressing place the oil, juice, harissa and garlic in a large jar and shake well to combine.
2. Put the couscous in a large bowl. Add 2/3 cup boiling water and set aside for 5 minutes for the water to be absorbed, then fluff up the couscous grains with a fork.
3. Add the chickpeas, green onions, tomatoes, mint and cilantro. Add the dressing and toss using two forks until the couscous is well coated.

NUTRITION PER SERVE (6)
Protein 10 g; Fat 15 g; Carbohydrate 30 g; Dietary Fiber 8 g; Cholesterol 0 mg; 300 calories

Notes: Harissa is a fiery chili paste used extensively in North African cooking. It is sold in tubes or jars in Middle Eastern markets.
    Couscous is a cereal product made from semolina, steamed and coated with flour.

Carrot and Pea Timbales

Ready to eat in 30 minutes
Serves 4

1 large carrot
2 eggs
1 2/3 cups frozen peas, thawed
1 onion, shredded
6 oz ricotta cheese
1/2 cup grated Parmesan
10 oz young spinach, trimmed
fresh flat-leaf parsley sprigs, to garnish

1. Preheat the oven to 425°F. Lightly grease four 1 cup capacity baking cups or ramekins. Peel the carrot, then peel thin ribbons from the carrot using a vegetable peeler and press the ribbons into each cup as a lining.
2. Combine the eggs, peas, onion, ricotta cheese and Parmesan in a bowl; season with pepper. Spoon into the cups, pressing down with the back of the spoon. Bake for 20–25 minutes, or until the timbales are puffed and set.
3. Meanwhile, bring a large pan of water to a boil and add the spinach. Cook until the spinach has just wilted. Drain the spinach and refresh under cold running water, then drain on paper towels.
4. Run a small knife around the inside of the cups to release the timbales. Place a bed of spinach on 4 serving plates, turn the timbales out onto the spinach, garnish with the flat-leaf parsley and serve immediately.

NUTRITION PER SERVE
Protein 20 g; Fat 15 g; Carbohydrate 6 g; Dietary Fiber 6 g; Cholesterol 125 mg; 210 calories

Chickpeas and Couscous with Harissa (top) with Carrot and Pea Timbales

Potatoes, Pronto!

Baby Potato Skins

Halve 1 lb new potatoes and cook in plenty of boiling water for 7 minutes, or until just tender. Drain and cool slightly, then scoop out the flesh, leaving 1/4 inch in the skins. Cut in half again. Meanwhile, heat 3/4 inch oil in a skillet.

Fry the skins in batches for 3–5 minutes, or until crisp and golden. Drain on paper towels, sprinkle with salt and serve with sour cream and sweet chili sauce. Serve with salad for a light meal.
Ready to eat in 25 minutes. Serves 4

NUTRITION PER SERVE
Protein 3 g; Fat 15 g; Carbohydrate 20 g; Dietary Fiber 2 g; Cholesterol 6.5 mg; 235 calories

Potato Galette

Thinly slice 1 lb 4 oz small potatoes. Heat 1 tablespoon butter and 1 tablespoon oil in a small skillet. Add the potato slices, slightly overlapping in thin layers. Cover and cook for 10 minutes. Over the sink, carefully invert a plate over the pan and turn out the potatoes. Slide the galette back into the pan and cook the other

From left to right: Baby Potato Skins; Potato Galette; Potato Salad with Roast Garlic Dressing

side, uncovered, for
5 minutes. Top with
2 sliced tomatoes and
sprinkle with 1/4 cup
finely shredded
Cheddar. Broil under a
preheated broiler until
the cheese is melted
and golden. Cut the
frittata into wedges
and serve.
*Ready to eat in
30 minutes. Serves 4*

NUTRITION PER SERVE
*Protein 6.5 g; Fat 10 g;
Carbohydrate 25 g; Dietary
Fiber 3 g; Cholesterol
20 mg; 225 calories*

Potato Salad with Roast Garlic Dressing

Preheat the oven to
450°F. Cut 1 lb finger
or old potatoes and
12 oz sweet potato
into small cubes. Put
in a baking dish with
10 garlic cloves.
Drizzle the vegetables
with 2 tablespoons
olive oil, sprinkle with
salt and pepper and
toss to combine. Roast
for 20 minutes, shaking
the pan a few times.

Peel the roast garlic
and place in a small
food processor with
1 egg, 2 teaspoons
white wine vinegar
and 1 teaspoon coarse-
grain mustard. Process
until smooth. With the
motor running, slowly
pour in 1/4 cup olive
oil. Add the dressing
to the potatoes with
2 tablespoons chopped
fresh parsley. Toss
gently and serve.
*Ready to eat in
30 minutes. Serves 4*

NUTRITION PER SERVE
*Protein 6.5 g; Fat 25 g;
Carbohydrate 30 g; Dietary
Fiber 5 g; Cholesterol
45 mg; 380 calories*

Gnocchi with Leek and Herb Sauce

*Ready to eat in
25 minutes
Serves 4–6*

2 tablespoons olive
oil
1 leek, thinly sliced
1 clove garlic,
crushed
16 oz can crushed
tomatoes
1/2 cup dry white wine
or water
1/2 cup semi-dried
tomatoes, chopped
1/2 cup chopped fresh
parsley
1/2 cup chopped fresh
basil
1 lb 4 oz fresh potato
gnocchi
grated Parmesan, to
serve

1. Heat the oil in a large saucepan. Add the leek and garlic and cook over medium heat for 5 minutes, or until they soften. Add the crushed tomatoes and wine and cook for 10 minutes longer, stirring often. Add a little water if the sauce is too thick. Stir in the semi-dried tomatoes and herbs.
2. Meanwhile, cook the gnocchi in a large saucepan of boiling water for 3–4 minutes, or until they rise to the surface, taking care not to overcook them. Drain in a colander.
3. Place the gnocchi in a large serving bowl, pour the sauce over the top and sprinkle with the Parmesan.

NUTRITION PER SERVE (6)
*Protein 10 g; Fat 15 g;
Carbohydrate 10 g; Dietary
Fiber 2 g; Cholesterol
40 mg; 240 calories*

Creamy Polenta with Three-cheese Sauce

*Ready to eat in
20 minutes
Serves 4*

1 1/2 cups instant
polenta
1/2 cup whipping
cream
1/2 cup grated
Parmesan, and extra,
for sprinkling
8 oz mascarpone
cheese
4 oz blue cheese,
crumbled
24 arugula leaves
3/4 cup walnut pieces
1 tablespoon fresh
oregano leaves
1 tablespoon fresh
marjoram leaves
1 tablespoon fresh sage
leaves

1. Bring 4 cups of water to a boil in a large heavy-based saucepan. Add the polenta in a slow stream, constantly stirring with a whisk. Reduce the heat and simmer for 2–5 minutes, stirring constantly. Remove from the heat and stir in the cream and Parmesan. Cover and set aside.
2. Gently melt the mascarpone in a small saucepan. Add half the blue cheese and cook for 1 minute, or until the cheese is melted.
3. Preheat the broiler to high. Place 6 arugula leaves on 4 ovenproof plates. Spoon the polenta into the middle and pour some sauce on top. Sprinkle with the remaining blue cheese, walnuts, herbs and Parmesan. Broil for 1 minute, or until light brown. Serve at once.

NUTRITION PER SERVE
*Protein 25 g; Fat 60 g;
Carbohydrate 40 g; Dietary
Fiber 3 g; Cholesterol
140 mg; 825 calories*

Notes: Instant polenta is sold in delicatessens and some supermarkets. The cooking time varies from 2–5 minutes.
Mascarpone is a fresh, unripened soft cream cheese available in major supermarkets.

*Creamy Polenta with Three-cheese Sauce (top)
and Gnocchi with Leek and Herb Sauce*

Pizza Perfect

Cook the pizzas in an oven preheated to 425°F.

Tomato Spread

Mix a crushed garlic clove and $1/2$ teaspoon of dried oregano into $1/3$ cup tomato paste. Spread over the pizza base and add your choice of topping.

Chargrilled Vegie Pizza with Feta

Place 1 large pizza base on a baking sheet. Spread with 1 quantity of Tomato Spread and sprinkle with $3/4$ cup shredded mozzarella. Top with 4 oz sliced chargrilled eggplant, 4 oz sliced chargrilled sweet bell pepper and 3 drained and sliced marinated artichokes. Sprinkle with 3 oz crumbled feta cheese and $1/2$ teaspoon dried oregano. Bake for 10–15 minutes, or until the cheese is golden. Serve at once.
Ready to eat in 30 minutes. Serves 2

NUTRITION PER SERVE
Protein 40 g; Fat 25 g; Carbohydrate 10 g; Dietary Fiber 5 g; Cholesterol 70 mg; 475 calories

Note: Delicatessens sell chargrilled vegetables.

From left to right: Chargrilled Vegie Pizza with Feta; Mushroom and Tomato Pizza; Goat's Cheese and Chutney Pizza

Mushroom and Tomato Pizza

Place 2 small pizza bases on a baking sheet. Spread with 1 quantity of Tomato Spread and sprinkle with 3/4 cup shredded mozzarella. Top with 8 sliced green onions, 2 teaspoons capers, 5 oz sliced mushrooms, 4 oz halved cherry tomatoes and 10 black olives.

Bake for 10 minutes. Sprinkle with 1/4 cup shredded mozzarella and 1/2 cup grated Parmesan. Bake for 5 minutes or until the cheese has melted. Serve at once.
Ready to eat in 30 minutes. Serves 2

NUTRITION PER SERVE
Protein 35 g; Fat 25 g; Carbohydrate 10 g; Dietary Fiber 7 g; Cholesterol 70 mg; 360 calories

Goat's Cheese and Chutney Pizza

Put 2 small pizza bases on a large baking sheet. Spread with 1 quantity of Tomato Spread and 2 tablespoons tomato chutney. Sprinkle with 3/4 cup shredded mozzarella. Scatter with 3 sliced green onions, 2 sliced tomatoes, 2/3 cup crumbled goat's cheese and 1 tablespoon shredded fresh basil. Bake for 15 minutes. Dot with about 2 tablespoons bottled pesto and a few small fresh basil leaves. Serve the pizzas at once.
Ready to eat in 30 minutes. Serves 2

NUTRITION PER SERVE
Protein 30 g; Fat 30 g; Carbohydrate 15 g; Dietary Fiber 5 g; Cholesterol 70 mg; 540 calories

Vegetable Pies

*Ready to eat in
30 minutes
Makes 4*

1 sheet ready-rolled
  puff pastry
1 egg, lightly
  beaten
4 green onions,
  chopped
2 cups shredded
  carrot
1 cup chopped
  broccoli
3/4 cup frozen
  peas
10 oz can creamed
  corn
2 eggs, lightly
  beaten
1/4 cup instant
  couscous
1/4 cup shredded
  Cheddar
1/2 cup grated
  Parmesan

1. Preheat the oven to
425°F. Have ready four
1 cup ramekins.
2. Cut 4 pastry circles
slightly larger than the
ramekins. Pierce with a
fork, brush with some
egg and place on a
parchment paper-lined
baking sheet. Bake for
10 minutes, or until gold
and puffy. Reduce the
oven to 350°F.
3. Meanwhile, combine
the other ingredients in
a bowl. Divide among
the ramekins, press
firmly and smooth the
top, and bake for
15 minutes. Serve with
the pastry on top.

NUTRITION PER SERVE
*Protein 20 g; Fat 20 g;
Carbohydrate 40 g; Dietary
Fiber 8 g; Cholesterol
165 mg; 425 calories*

Note: To cook the pies
in the microwave, cover
with paper towels and
microwave on High
(100%) for 3 minutes.
Rest for 1 minute, cook
for 3 minutes, then rest
for 1 minute. Cook for
2–3 minutes more, or
until cooked and set.

Lentils with Lime-yogurt Dressing

*Ready to eat in
25 minutes
Serves 6*

1 tablespoon olive oil
1 large onion,
  chopped
2 cloves garlic,
  crushed
1 teaspoon grated fresh
  ginger
1/4 teaspoon garam
  masala
1 tablespoon hot curry
  powder
1 carrot, chopped
3 cups vegetable stock
2 cups red lentils
6 naan breads
2 tablespoons cilantro
  leaves

Lime-yogurt Dressing
1 cup plain yogurt
1 tablespoon lime juice
1 green onion, finely
  chopped

1. Heat the oil in a
saucepan, add the
onion and cook for
2 minutes, or until it
starts to soften. Add
the garlic, ginger, spices
and carrot and stir for
1 minute. Preheat the
broiler to low.
2. Add the stock and
lentils to the pan. Bring
to a boil, then reduce
the heat and simmer,
without stirring, for
8 minutes, or until the
lentils are tender.
3. Meanwhile, broil the
naan until warm and
crusty. Combine the
ingredients for the lime-
yogurt dressing.
4. To serve, spoon the
lentils onto the naan
and sprinkle with
cilantro. Top with a
dollop of the dressing.

NUTRITION PER SERVE
*Protein 50 g; Fat 45 g;
Carbohydrate 190 g; Dietary
Fiber 15 g; Cholesterol
5 mg; 395 calories*

Note: For softer lentils,
add 3/4 cup vegetable
stock to the lentils and
cook for 4–5 minutes
longer, or until the
liquid is absorbed.

*Vegetable Pies (top) and
Lentils with Lime-yogurt Dressing*

Fettuccine with Cilantro and Carrot Pesto

*Ready to eat in
25 minutes*
Serves 4

1 lb fresh fettuccine or
  linguine
$1/2$ cup olive oil
1 onion, chopped
1 clove garlic, chopped
$2/3$ cup pine nuts
10 oz carrots, chopped
  (see Note)
1 cup cilantro leaves
  and stems
$1^1/2$ cups fresh flat-leaf
  parsley
1 teaspoon salt
1 teaspoon freshly
  ground black pepper
$3/4$ cup grated
  Parmesan

1. Cook the pasta in
a large saucepan of
boiling water for
5 minutes, or until
just tender. Drain and
keep warm.
2. Meanwhile, heat
2 tablespoons of the oil
in a skillet. Add the
onion and garlic; cover
and cook over medium
heat for 4 minutes.
3. Add the pine nuts
and cook, uncovered,
for 2 minutes, stirring
occasionally. Increase
the heat to high. Add
the carrot, stir well,
then cover and cook
for 2 minutes.
4. Transfer the carrot
mixture to a food
processor. Add the
cilantro, parsley, salt,
pepper, remaining oil
and half the cheese,
then process until
just combined.
5. Divide the pasta
among serving bowls.
Top with the carrot
pesto and toss gently.
Sprinkle with the rest
of the cheese and serve.

NUTRITION PER SERVE
*Protein 25 g; Fat 55 g;
Carbohydrate 95 g; Dietary
Fiber 10 g; Cholesterol
20 mg; 970 calories*

Note: You will not need
to peel the carrots.

Sweet Squash and Marmalade Curry

*Ready to eat in
30 minutes*
Serves 4

2 tablespoons oil
1 onion, chopped
2 tablespoons mild
  Indian curry paste
1 teaspoon ground
  cumin
1 teaspoon ground
  turmeric
2 lb butternut squash,
  peeled and coarsely
  chopped
2 new potatoes,
  unpeeled, cut into
  bite-size pieces
1 cup vegetable stock
1 tablespoon orange
  marmalade
1 tablespoon lime
  juice
1 teaspoon soft brown
  sugar
2 tablespoons
  unsweetened coconut
  cream
6 oz baby bok choy
  (Chinese white
  cabbage), halved
  lengthwise
cilantro leaves, to
  garnish

1. In a large deep
saucepan, heat the oil.
Add the onion, curry
paste, cumin and
turmeric. Cover and
cook over medium heat
for about 5 minutes.
2. Add the squash,
potatoes, vegetable
stock and marmalade.
Cover and cook
over high heat for
12 minutes.
3. Stir in the lime juice,
sugar and coconut
cream. Place the bok
choy on top. Cover and
cook for 2–3 minutes,
or until the bok choy
is just tender. Garnish
with cilantro leaves
and serve.

NUTRITION PER SERVE
*Protein 8 g; Fat 15 g;
Carbohydrate 30 g; Dietary
Fiber 4.5 g; Cholesterol
0 mg; 300 calories*

*Fettuccine with Cilantro and Carrot Pesto (top)
and Sweet Squash and Marmalade Curry*

Cashew-nut Tarts

Ready to eat in
25 minutes
Serves 4

2 sheets ready-rolled
puff pastry
1/4 cup cashew nut
spread
1/4 cup fresh basil
leaves
10 small marinated
artichokes, drained
and coarsely chopped
6 oz mixed antipasto
vegetables

1. Preheat the oven to 425°F. Lightly grease two baking sheets. Cut each pastry sheet into 4 squares and pierce all over with a fork.
2. Place the pastry squares on the baking sheets and bake for 8 minutes, or until golden and well risen. Allow to cool slightly, then spread with the cashew nut spread.
3. Gently mix together the basil leaves, artichokes and mixed vegetables. Arrange the mixture over the pastry squares and serve at once with a salad for a light lunch or as an appetizer for an evening meal.

NUTRITION PER SERVE
Protein 10 g; Fat 25 g;
Carbohydrate 35 g; Dietary
Fiber 6 g; Cholesterol
20 mg; 420 calories

Note: Cashew nut spread is available from health food shops.

Mushroom and Brown Rice Casserole

Ready to eat in
30 minutes
Serves 4–6

3 slices thick toast
bread, crusts
removed
1/4 cup olive oil
2 onions,
chopped
12 oz flat mushrooms,
chopped
14 oz can crushed
tomatoes
2 teaspoons sweet
paprika
2 teaspoons mixed
dried herbs
1/2 teaspoon sugar
2 cups cooked brown
rice (see Note)
1/3 cup vegetable
stock
1/4 cup pine nuts
2 tablespoons chopped
fresh flat-leaf
parsley

1. Preheat the oven to 425°F. Cut each slice of bread into 4 triangles.
2. Heat 1 tablespoon of the oil in a skillet, add the onions and mushrooms and toss over high heat for 2 minutes, or until the mushrooms have softened. Add the tomatoes, paprika, herbs and sugar. Bring to a boil, reduce the heat and simmer for about 2 minutes, or until thickened slightly. Add the rice and stock; mix well. Season with salt and freshly ground black pepper.
3. Spoon the mixture into a 6 cup capacity baking dish and overlap the bread on top. Drizzle with the remaining oil and sprinkle with the pine nuts. Bake for about 10 minutes, or until the bread is browned and crusty. Sprinkle with the chopped parsley to serve.

NUTRITION PER SERVE (6)
Protein 10 g; Fat 15 g;
Carbohydrate 60 g; Dietary
Fiber 6 g; Cholesterol
0 mg; 435 calories

Notes: To obtain the right amount of rice for this recipe, you will need to cook about 1 cup brown rice.

This recipe can be made up to 3 hours ahead and baked just before serving to heat the casserole through and brown the crust.

Cashew-nut Tarts (top)
with Mushroom and Brown Rice Casserole

Index